Warring
Mental Warfare

WARRING MENTAL WARFARE

Mark T. Barclay

All scripture references are quoted from the
King James Version of the Holy Bible
unless otherwise noted.

First Printing 1996

ISBN 0-944802-28-1

Write:
Mark Barclay Ministries
P.O. Box 588, Midland, MI 48640-0588

CONTENTS

CHAPTER 1
SPIRIT, SOUL, AND BODY

One of the very first things to learn is that you are a human, a man, and God created you in His image. The very basic image of God is that He is triune in being. He is a three-part being yet He is one. You could say that He has three parts that make up His person. Some scholars say that He has three personalities that work so closely together that they are one. God is Jehovah Creator, Word, and Spirit (also referred to as Father, Son, and Holy Ghost).

We (mankind) are created like Him, in His likeness. We also are three parts yet one man/woman. We are made in the very basic image of God. Man is a spirit, he has a soul, and he lives in a body (spirit, soul, and body yet one creature—man). God created us this way so we would resemble Him.

> "And God said, Let us make man in our **image**, after our likeness: and let them have dominion over the fish of the sea, and over the fowl of the air, and over the cattle, and over all the earth, and over every creeping thing that creepeth upon the earth.
>
> So God created man in his own image, in the image of God created he him; male and female created he them."
>
> Genesis 1:26-27

*"And the very God of peace sanctify you wholly; and I pray God your whole **spirit and soul and body** be preserved blameless unto the coming of our Lord Jesus Christ."*

1 Thessalonians 5:23

YOUR BODY

Let's talk about your body first because it is the part of man that most people understand the most. The body is the house or tent that you live in. Your body has parts and life to it. The parts are obvious—your arms, legs, head, organs, and so on. Your body has life to it. We call that your five senses (that is, your nose system to smell, your mouth system to taste, your ear system to hear, your touch system to feel, and your eye system to see).

Of course your body also has a skin covering, hair, and an immune system to protect you from anti-life elements that you may encounter while on this earth. You cannot survive and live on earth without your body. Every man only gets one, and it must last you the duration of your time here on this planet.

Paul called it a tent.

*"For we know that if our earthly house of this **tabernacle** were dissolved, we have a building of God, an house not made with hands, eternal in the heavens.*

For in this we groan, earnestly desiring to be clothed upon with our house which is from heaven:

If so be that being clothed we shall not be found naked.

For we that are in this tabernacle do groan, being

2

burdened: not for that we would be unclothed, but clothed upon, that mortality might be swallowed up of life.

Now he that hath wrought us for the selfsame thing is God, who also hath given unto us the earnest of the Spirit.

Therefore we are always confident, knowing that, whilst we are at home in the body, we are absent from the Lord . . ."

2 Corinthians 5:1-6

Jesus taught us that this tabernacle (tent) would be changed into a mansion. Imagine that! As good looking as you are in this life, you will become so much more beautiful—I mean the difference between a tent and a mansion! That's a significant face-lift.

*"In my Father's house are many **mansions**: if it were not so, I would have told you. I go to prepare a place for you."*

John 14:2

Paul wrote that we would be changed in the twinkling of an eye and that we would put on this new body.

"And as we have borne the image of the earthy, we shall also bear the image of the heavenly.

Now this I say, brethren, that flesh and blood cannot inherit the kingdom of God; neither doth corruption inherit incorruption.

Behold, I shew you a mystery; We shall not all sleep, but we shall all be changed,

*In a moment, in the **twinkling** of an eye, at the last trump: for the trumpet shall sound, and the dead*

3

shall be raised incorruptible, and we shall be changed.

For this corruptible must put on incorruption, and this mortal must put on immortality.

So when this corruptible shall have put on incorruption, and this mortal shall have put on immortality, then shall be brought to pass the saying that is written, Death is swallowed up in victory."

1 Corinthians 15:49-54

But for now I must bring you back to reality of this life and remind you that you still are bound to this earth suit, your fleshly body.

YOUR SOUL

Let's talk about your soul. Your soul we'll say is the layer that is between your body and your innermost being, your spirit. Remember you are a spirit, you have a soul, and you live in a body.

Just like your body has parts (e.g., arms and legs), so does your soul. Your soul is known as your personality. It is made up of your mind (your intellect, your thinking faculties, your ability to reason, and your storage tank for remembering and recalling data), your emotions (your feelings and your ability to express them), and your volition (your willpower and choice).

You cannot survive and live on earth without your soul. Every man only gets one, and it must last you the duration of your time here on this planet. Most of this book is written about how to deal with your soul.

Jesus taught about the soul. Read the following scripture:

*"For what is a man profited, if he shall gain the whole world, and lose his own **soul**? or what shall a man give in exchange for his **soul**?"*

Matthew 16:26

Paul also taught us about our soul:

"I beseech you therefore, brethren, by the mercies of God, that ye present your bodies a living sacrifice, holy, acceptable unto God, which is your reasonable service.

And be not conformed to this world: but be ye transformed by the renewing of your mind, that ye may prove what is that good, and acceptable, and perfect will of God."

Romans 12:1-2

*"But we are not of them who draw back unto perdition; but of them that believe to the **saving of the soul**."*

Hebrews 10:39

John even gives us insight into the soul and its prospering.

*"Beloved, I wish above all things that thou mayest prosper and be in health, even as thy **soul** prospereth."*

3 John 1:2

You must realize that when you were born again only your spirit man was regenerated. You must work out your own salvation (that is, the saving of the soul) so that you can see Heaven.

YOUR SPIRIT

You cannot survive and live on earth without your

5

spirit. Every man only gets one, and it is you for the duration of your time here on this planet, as well as for eternity. You are a spirit. If you are born again and regenerated by the Spirit of God, then you are constantly bearing witness with His Spirit and His with yours (Rom. 8:16).

Your spirit is the innermost part of your being. Your life center is here. God intended for your whole system to be run by your spirit. You are the temple of the Holy Ghost, and this is the part of you that houses Him. You could say in a sense that you and God live in your innermost being (John 7:38, 1 Cor. 3:16-17).

Your regenerated spirit man wants to work hand in hand with your body and your soul to make you a well-disciplined, totally-scriptural, wholesome being. Because it is your spirit man that mostly and constantly bears witness with God's Spirit, it (actually you) will always know what is right and best for you and will try to lead you by communicating to your soul. It works through the system of bearing witness, discerning, and what some call intuition.

Even though many men have tried to explain the conscience, all have sufficiently failed it seems. I believe the conscience is the voice of your spirit man. Just like your soul has a voice (emotions and attitudes) and your body has a voice (comfort, pain, and other feelings), so your spirit man has a voice. I see it as the inner voice that talks to you often and helps you sort out the values and principles of life (Rom. 2:15).

Again I remind you that this particular book is about your soul, for we are zeroing in on "mental warfare."

CHAPTER 2
THE ENEMIES OF YOUR SOUL

*"Dearly beloved, I beseech you as strangers and pilgrims, abstain from fleshly lusts, which **war against the soul** . . ."*

1 Peter 2:11

In the last chapter we studied the three-part makeup of man—that he was created in the image of God and that he is a spirit, he has a soul, and he lives in a body. He is three parts yet one man.

Everyone knows that your body has enemies. It must fight these enemies and conquer them in order to live. One must win, whether it be a war against sickness, disease, virus, bacteria, or another living thing. Your body can get injured and maimed by an accident (God forbid). You have enemies to your body that can harm you and even shorten or extinguish your life.

Just as your body has enemies, so does your spirit man. The Bible says that a wounded spirit is hard to bear (Prov. 18:14).

Your spirit can be affected by a human spirit, a hellish spirit, or the Holy Spirit. A human spirit can severely harm you and even take your life. A hellish spirit can seduce, deceive, torment, agitate, and stir up your entire environment. Some people are actually to the point of demon possession. Unforgiveness can cause a root of bitterness that can ruin your entire life.

Just like your body and your spirit have enemies, so does your soul. Your soul is as real as the rest of you. Remember what I taught in chapter 1, that your soul is made up of your emotions, attitudes, feelings, intellect, and your choice or will. Just like your body gives you—the spirit—mobility, so does your soul give you "personality."

There are many enemies to your soul. For example, there is confusion, frustration, worry, fear, doubt, unbelief, depression, discouragement, etc. You must war against these enemies because they are as lethal as any other enemies of life. They have the potential to shorten your life, if not extinguish it.

We preachers have taught you well how to war against the spiritual enemies and to protect yourself from the things that can harm your body, but we have been weak at teaching you how to do mental warfare. (As a preacher myself, I have a right to say this.)

You live in a really dark and dangerous day. You must be quick to discern the tricks and snares of the wicked one. You must be equipped with scriptural weapons and know how to use them if you are going to live a life with any peace at all.

Following is a brief list of some of the enemies of your soul and how some people in the Bible were affected by these enemies.

Enemies of Your Soul	Bible Examples	Outcome
Pride	Aaron/Miriam	Trouble with God
Fear	King Saul	Disobeyed God
Arrogance	Absalom	It killed him
Discouragement	David	Lived distressed
Lust	David	Murdered for Bathsheba
Worry	Martha (Luke 10:41) Children of Israel	Many pains, sorrows, and deaths
Confusion	Judas Iscariot	Caused him to betray
Suicide	Judas Iscariot	Went for money Killed himself
Frustration	Barnabas	Separated from Paul over John Mark
Depression	Elijah	Prayed to die
Belligerence	Herod	Died of worms
Know-it-all	Peter	Denied Christ
Doubt	Thomas	Marked his life forever
Worldliness	Simon the Sorcerer	Tried to buy his way in the ministry
Independence	Eve	Betrayed the human race
Passiveness	Solomon	Allowed his wife to worship false gods

There are more, my friend—many, many more.

*"Dearly beloved, I beseech you as strangers and pilgrims, abstain from fleshly lusts, which **war against the soul** . . ."*

1 Peter 2:11

CHAPTER 3
HEARTS WEIGHED DOWN
AND FAILING

"That I have great heaviness and continual sorrow in my heart."

Romans 9:2 (The apostle Paul)

There are many things in this life that are designed to burden your heart, affect your emotions, and even depress you. Living in these last days is like living in a pressure cooker. That's right, a pressure cooker. People everywhere, even Christians, seem to be looking for a place to let off steam. Even if you do everything right, you still can live under stress and constant fear (e.g., fear of failure, crime, abuse, poverty, and rejection).

Humans have emotions. Even Jesus showed His emotional side once in a while. Even Jesus at times felt burdened and heavy in heart and mind. Even Jesus had to deal with the pressures of life—its troubles and its enemies.

Study this scripture for a while. Let it get in your soul. It seems as though we are being advised that troubled hearts and minds are our choice.

*"That ye be not soon shaken in mind, or be **troubled**,*

neither by spirit, nor by word, nor by letter as from us, as that the day of Christ is at hand."

2 Thessalonians 2:2

Be not shaken. This is a command it seems, not just a suggestion. There must be a Bible way to stay free from the damaging effect of even today's pressures.

In the scripture above, the Holy Spirit reveals to us that we can be shaken in mind and troubled by three different causes. We can be shaken by spirits, by words, and by written communications.

We must protect our hearts from evil spirits as well as humans who have seducing spirits. Other humans can get you down just by being around them. I'm not suggesting you isolate yourself or hibernate. I am, however, advising you to be choosy who your friends are and whom you allow in your life. Humans are carriers. They can carry diseases, sicknesses, strife, doubt, unbelief, fear, worry, and many other things that can affect your soul. These elements protruding from and being emitted from other humans can have a very severe, negative effect on you and can even change you to the worse. Of course humans can be carriers of good, wholesome things as well.

There are also evil, deceiving, and seducing spirits. They don't always use human vessels to deal with you. They can infiltrate your life through thoughts and influences and strange means of communications.

You could be brought to a low degree by a letter or by what you read and look at. Reading and watching are two of satan's most powerful ways to infiltrate your life to do harm. Watch carefully what you read, and use great discretion in what you see on TV and at the movies. I can promise you that even if you are strong, these things can be an avenue for ill emotions to enter in.

Many people awaken in the morning with troubled minds and feelings. I believe a lot of this has to do with what they watched or read before they went to sleep. Your mind doesn't always rest while your body is. You may expect to rest your body and feel strong in the morning or after a nap, but if your mind harassed you during your sleep, you will not be strong. There is too great a contact and relation between your mind and the rest of your being.

Surely by now with all the teaching we've had, we know how to monitor whom and what we listen to. Conversation can be the cannon shot by satan that does you in (if not totally, then at least messing with your well-being). Many people who are doing good can be poisoned and bombed by the conversation of another. One must be discerning because it isn't always the way it's said but what is said. At times it's just the opposite—it isn't what is said but the way it's implied.

Even Jesus had to deal with things. He groaned inside of Himself and He wept, and even His soul was troubled at times. If Jesus had to deal with a troubled soul, you need to find out how He dealt with it because you are no super human.

> *"When Jesus therefore saw her weeping, and the Jews also weeping which came with her, he **GROANED** in the spirit, and was troubled . . ."*
>
> John 11:33

> *"**NOW IS MY SOUL TROUBLED**; and what shall I say? Father, save me from this hour: but for this cause came I unto this hour."*
>
> John 12:27

Sin, riotous living, peeking at pornography, gossiping, skipping church, and denying prayer and Bible study can be the very things that overcharge your inner man and start to cause you weariness and fatigue. Especially in these last days we need to stay with Kingdom strengths and not let the world and its ways or practices wear us down.

Notice that the scripture following warns us of things that can overcharge or overwhelm your heart. I might point out that most of us have beaten such things as drunkenness and surfeiting, but all of us must deal with the affairs of this life.

> *"And take heed to yourselves, lest at any time your hearts be overcharged with surfeiting, and drunkenness, and cares of this life, and so that day come upon you unawares."*

Luke 21:34

> *"Wherefore God also gave them up to uncleanness through the lusts of their own hearts, to dishonor their own bodies between themselves . . ."*

Romans 1:24

> *"Who changed the truth of God into a lie, and worshiped and served the creature more than the Creator, who is blessed for ever. Amen."*

Romans 1:25

> *"And he said unto them, Why are ye troubled? and why do thoughts arise in your hearts?"*

Luke 24:38

Many times people have such a draw (lust or want) for something or someone that they allow that lust to literally catch them up and carry them away. Even the strongest among us will suffer fainting and pain if we allow this to happen. No one, not one of us, should flirt with the world or behave like we belong to it. Refuse to be tainted or defiled, and you will not be scarred or maimed. Daniel purposed in his heart not to be defiled.

This is why I preach so much on right-living. I see a direct connection between wrong-living and one's attitude and emotional state. It's like a car pulling another car with a tow hitch. The car behind is forced to follow the one with the power. Don't allow yourself to get to this place. If you have, then go see your church leaders ASAP.

> *"For consider him that endured such contradiction of sinners against himself, lest ye be wearied and **faint** in your minds."*
>
> Hebrews 12:3

> *"For which cause we **faint** not; but though our outward man perish, yet the inward man is renewed day by day."*
>
> 2 Corinthians 4:16

CHAPTER 4
DIAGNOSIS BEFORE TREATMENT

We Christians are the strangest beings on planet earth and probably the most superstitious at times. We are so afraid of being dealt with and whether or not we are received by others. This feeling of insecurity and inferiority may actually be the height of the pride that came out of Adam and Eve's tree-eating experience. Nonetheless, it is a real robber of the human being.

We are not at all hesitant to have our automobile diagnosed by a technician so we can locate the problem and apply accurate repairs. We all wish our cars would run without flaw, but they just don't seem to. Even strong faith people who know how to live right and trust God have to change their oil and make repairs to their vehicle once in a while.

The same is true with your body. It isn't comfortable to go to the doctor for tests and diagnostic work, but it is at times the wisest thing to do. It must make sense to most humans, because not only are the doctors among the busiest professionals but our hospitals are full.

We will allow the doctor to do diagnostic work to help us locate the problem so proper care can be prescribed. So goes the story of life.

I wonder why Christians, in fact all people for that matter, are so afraid to allow the preacher (God's technician) to do diagnostic work on the soul. Many people are paranoid of this kind of work. Why? If you will just allow the man or woman of God to help you (with the Scriptures), then you will be able to pinpoint your problem and deal with it precisely and accurately.

I live in the North. Michigan is where I was raised and now have my world headquarters. We can have some very severe winters and usually do. With this in mind I always give a favorite illustration of mine: Imagine that my family is traveling along a freshly snow-covered road on a subzero wintry day. As we buck the snow with our four-wheel drive vehicle, we come upon a car in a deep ditch. The driver had lost control and spun out, landing in the snowbank so severely that he couldn't manage to get out. My family and I slow down to notice this, and lo and behold, it's a family from our church. We are thrilled to see them and wave with all of our might. We don't stop for them but finish our drive in the snow.

If this really happened, this family would be furious with me. In fact they would be fighting mad. Everyone knows that this family could easily have died out there. Once that vehicle ran out of gas the heater wouldn't work anymore, and frost would have started its blistery work. Listen to me, this condition could be very fatal for this family. I wouldn't blame them at all for being irate with me. I could have saved the entire family, but I just kept right on going.

Why is it, I wonder, that this same family that would be so outraged about me not helping them out of an adverse dangerous physical condition would get irate to the same degree if I tried to stop and help them out of a lethal soulful or spiritual condition. That's right—many people get vein-bulging mad if you try to save them and their family from spiritual deception or seduction.

In the natural situation they will call you names and accuse you of heartlessness if you drive by their car in the ditch. The same people will treat you the same way if you stop to help them save themselves and their family in the spiritual or soulful arenas. It seems as though the devil has severely indoctrinated us in these matters. Let's break out of his control and go to the men and women of God in these days and allow them to help us.

Many times believers who are skilled in hermeneutics can diagnose their own problem by self-examination through the Holy Scriptures. I have found though that most Christians are so busy with life's affairs and duties that their study of the Bible has suffered because of it (to the degree of great danger). This is where it pays to have a good general practitioner preacher in your life who knows you and your style of living.

A heart surgeon told me once that his daddy raised him with the principle that you cannot be a success in this world without a good doctor, a good lawyer, and a good preacher.

Part of the preacher's job description from God is to help you diagnose what is ailing you soulfully and spiritually and prescribe the right treatment.

Study and meditate in these scriptures for yourself. May they change your view of things and spare your life as well as your family's.

"If thou put the brethren in remembrance of these things, thou shalt be a good minister of Jesus Christ, nourished up in the words of faith and of good doctrine, whereunto thou hast attained."

1 Timothy 4:6

"I charge thee therefore before God, and the Lord Jesus Christ, who shall judge the quick and the dead at his appearing and his kingdom;

Preach the word; be instant in season, out of season; reprove, rebuke, exhort with all longsuffering and doctrine.

For the time will come when they will not endure sound doctrine; but after their own lusts shall they heap to themselves teachers, having itching ears;

And they shall turn away their ears from the truth, and shall be turned unto fables.

But watch thou in all things, endure afflictions, do the work of an evangelist, make full proof of thy ministry."

2 Timothy 4:1-5

"Obey them that have the rule over you, and submit yourselves: for they watch for your souls, as they that must give account, that they may do it with joy, and not with grief: for that is unprofitable for you."

Hebrews 13:17

"For the word of God is quick, and powerful, and sharper than any twoedged sword, piercing even to the dividing asunder of soul and spirit, and of the joints and marrow, and is a discerner of the thoughts and intents of the heart."

Hebrews 4:12

"My son, forget not my law; but let thine heart keep my commandments:

20

For length of days, and long life, and peace, shall they add to thee."

Proverbs 3:1-2

"But if all prophesy, and there come in one that believeth not, or one unlearned, he is convinced of all, he is judged of all:

And thus are the secrets of his heart made manifest; and so falling down on his face he will worship God, and report that God is in you of a truth."

1 Corinthians 14:24-25

*"For the preaching of the cross is to them that perish, **foolishness**; but unto us which are saved it is the power of God.*

For it is written, I will destroy the wisdom of the wise, and will bring to nothing the understanding of the prudent.

Where is the wise? where is the scribe? where is the disputer of this world? hath not God made foolish the wisdom of this world?

For after that in the wisdom of God the world by wisdom knew not God, it pleased God by the foolishness of preaching to save them that believe."

1 Corinthians 1:18-21

Constantly the New Testament is revealing to us that it is the job of the preacher to instruct us how to live right and to show us the way of salvation. This is not always comfortable but usually absolutely necessary for a long wholesome life and protected family. Search the Scriptures further for more revelation on the importance of being ministered to consistently by an anointed gospel minister.

Listen friend, your car will clunk and bang only so

long before it breaks down. That unusual noise doesn't belong there. It was not put there by the creator of your car. If you don't get it diagnosed and fixed properly, you will pay for it later in a more severe way.

That malfunction in your body doesn't belong there. The pain is a sign of something wrong. If you don't get it diagnosed soon, it could turn into something big, something lethal. Your Creator didn't put it there as part of your normal operating system. You will pay a very dear price later for your procrastination now.

Mental warfare, depression, worry, pressure, and such do not belong to you. Your Creator did not put them in you as a normal operating function. Go to His Word and His preacher and get them diagnosed immediately. This could save you from dealing with fatal things later in your life or the lives of your loved ones.

CHAPTER 5
DON'T COPE WITH—CONQUER

*"Ye are of God, little children, and have **overcome** them: because greater is he that is in you, than he that is in the world."*

1 John 4:4

"But thanks be to God, which giveth us the victory through our Lord Jesus Christ."

1 Corinthians 15:57

*"For whatsoever is born of God **overcometh** the world: and this is the victory that **overcometh** the world, even our faith."*

1 John 5:4

"And I will say to my soul, Soul . . ."

Luke 12:19

This may seem strange to you, but nonetheless let me tell you. You have to learn to talk to yourself. That's right, talk to yourself. I don't mean to hold a conversation with yourself or to answer yourself. You have to learn to speak within yourself, to command your soul to respond, just like David did. He talked to his soul; that is, his inner man, his feelings, and his thoughts. He commanded his soul to bless the Lord. In fact he commanded all that was within him to bless the Lord.

> *"Bless the LORD, O my soul: and all that is within me, bless his holy name.*
>
> *Bless the LORD, O my soul, and forget not all his benefits . . ."*
>
> Psalm 103:1-2

There was a woman who had an issue of blood for 12 years, and she was weak and dying. The doctors did all they could, but she didn't get better. She had spent all her money seeking a cure but found none. In her desperate shape she decided to talk within herself. She convinced herself that Jesus could heal her. She followed her inner commands and was totally made whole.

If you'll stop and think about it for a moment, you'll realize that you have been talking within yourself all along but maybe not with the right counsel. Do you constantly rehearse all your troubles and meditate on the problems, or do you constantly bless the Lord and meditate on His Word?

> *"For she said **within herself**, If I may but touch his garment, I shall be whole.*
>
> *But Jesus turned him about, and when he saw her, he said, Daughter, be of good comfort; thy faith hath made thee whole. And the woman was made whole from that hour."*
>
> Matthew 9:21-22

It is the will of God for all New Testament Christians to be overcomers. More and more I find myself refusing to bow. As a new Christian, it seemed like I was pleased with myself just to make it through a tribulation or trial. It felt victorious just to say I didn't lose this one. But as I grew up in Christ, I realized that Jesus was not satisfied with us barely making it. He wants us to have the victory each and every time. He is not satisfied with our not burning in the furnace, but He wants to get us out of the furnace. Not to burn is one thing—coming out of the fiery trial is better yet.

Too many Christians are cutting themselves short of God's entire blessing for their life. How? By the cope-with attitude. We must learn to be dissatisfied with coping with the enemy and remain focused until we win. I'm no longer satisfied with stopping my enemies from destroying me. I want them out of my life!

The army of God learned to cope with the daily challenge of Goliath. He would rise from his nap, shake a fist at them, and spew out a few blasphemous words to provoke them to fight. They simply denied him the fight and went about the rest of the day hiding in holes. Many people live this way. They have not beaten their enemies at all and live in the pits because of it.

It's great that your Goliath didn't kill you today. That's a sense of relief all by itself. However it's not total victory. Getting out of the hole you have been living in and charging the enemy until he is defeated is the only real sense of victory.

Just like David did, you and I must stop hiding from the things we fear and go after them face-to-face. Was David at all afraid that day? I think so, but his faith was stronger. He wasn't daily seduced by the presence of this Goliath. He dealt with him immediately (you know the story I'm sure).

Shake no hands with the enemy. Do not negotiate at all. Do not fellowship with his presence or entertain his notions at all. You must get fed up with his very presence and aggressively go after him until you win. Anything short of this is coping with his presence.

We live in a world where we are taught to cope with things. Even the medical profession at times will teach someone to learn to live with something they cannot cure or cut out. One time a friend of mine was told, "You better learn to live with this because there is no cure for it, and you will have it the rest of your life." Well . . . he doesn't have it anymore. I'm glad he chose to fight it all the way instead getting psychiatric help to cope with it.

Coping with something is simply a way to find a peaceful place for you and it to dwell together. I'm not satisfied with this. Conquering is a mentality. It is a change and renewing of the mind. Very few people find this easy to do, and some even find it uncomfortable. Why? Because of the way we have thought all these years.

You probably have been programmed most of your life to accept certain things rather than exempt yourself from them. You will probably have trouble changing this way of life without the Word of God doing it for you.

Paul told us to press toward the mark. Go for the high prize. Don't settle for 10 years of life with a disease when you could believe for 35 years without it.

Years ago my car was running funny, and it even sounded abnormal. I had it diagnosed by a mechanic. He told me the problem and gave me two options for recovery. I could just let it go until it totally broke and then be forced to fix it, along with whatever else it damaged in its process, or I could fix it now and get it over with before it got any worse or wore out anything in its path. Today I would fix it and know that it isn't under that hood any longer. Back then I chose to wait. Do you know that every time I started that car I had to deal with the inner feeling that this may be the day that the thing totally goes out? Every noise I heard bothered me as I drove down the road.

One day that part finally wore out, and it cost me an arm and a leg to fix it. It not only went out, but the extra wear it put on the other parts that were carrying its load also cost me money and life on my car.

Listen, worse than not having the money to fix that car at the time was the daily doubt, fear, and worry that faced me every time I used that car. I knew that thing was there under the hood and would someday cost me money and probably leave me stranded.

I hope you are not a procrastinator. Procrastinators live miserable lives because they leave so many things undone in a day and then have to face them again the next day.

I remember when I was in the United States Marine Corps, and it was time for shots. They asked who wanted to go that day and who wanted to go the next day. The shots were not an option. The only option was the day to receive the inoculations. I chose that day. I didn't want to have those shots on the back of my mind all day and night long. I didn't want to go to bed with them on my mind, and they were the last thing that I wanted to wake up to in the morning. Wow, I hated those things! You had to go through a line, and they used needles and guns on both arms and legs as well as had you drink something. No way was I going to think about that all day long.

Once when I had to discipline my son Josh, I gave him

an option of when he wanted to go to the woodshed. "Son, you are going to get a spanking for this. Do you want me to do it right now while you have friends waiting outside for you, or do you want to wait until later?" He said, "There's no way, Dad, that I can wait. It would ruin my day if I tried to do anything while I waited for the woodshed. Do it now and get it over with."

Once when disciplining my daughter Dawn, I asked her if she wanted a spanking or to be grounded as her discipline. She chose the spanking, as much as she hated it, because she said it was better to face it and get it over with than to have to think about it for a few days.

Study the Scriptures along these lines and let them renew your mind. Make it easy for the Holy Spirit to teach you to go beyond "coping with" things and have an overcomer's attitude.

Here's a Barclay proverb: "As with your attitude, so goes your life." Barclay proverb #2: "Blessed are the flexible, for they shall not be broken."

Just because you don't win today doesn't mean you lose. Just because you didn't get your own way doesn't mean there is no way. Learn to roll with the punches a little bit until you win. You will win. It is the will of God in Christ Jesus concerning you.

> *"Who shall separate us from the love of Christ? shall tribulation, or distress, or persecution, or famine, or nakedness, or peril, or sword?*
>
> *As it is written, For thy sake we are killed all the day long; we are accounted as sheep for the slaughter.*
>
> *Nay, in all these things we are more than **conquerors***

through him that loved us.

For I am persuaded, that neither death, nor life, nor angels, nor principalities, nor powers, nor things present, nor things to come,

Nor height, nor depth, nor any other creature, shall be able to separate us from the love of God, which is in Christ Jesus our Lord."

Romans 8:35-39

"I write unto you, fathers, because ye have known him that is from the beginning. I write unto you, young men, because ye have overcome the wicked one. I write unto you, little children, because ye have known the Father."

1 John 2:13

"Therefore, my beloved brethren, be ye STEDFAST, unmovable, always abounding in the work of the Lord, forasmuch as ye know that your labour is not in vain in the Lord."

1 Corinthians 15:58

*"He that hath an ear, let him hear what the Spirit saith unto the churches; To him that **overcometh** will I give to eat of the tree of life, which is in the midst of the paradise of God."*

Revelation 2:7

CHAPTER 6
I DROP THE CHARGES

*"Let all **bitterness**, and wrath, and anger, and clamour, and evil speaking, be put away from you, with all malice:*

And be ye kind one to another, tenderhearted, forgiving one another, even as God for Christ's sake hath forgiven you."

Ephesians 4:31-32

Unforgiveness easily could be the largest life robber in the Body of Christ today. It steals your joy, disturbs your peace, and can literally make you physically sick. Unforgiveness can totally consume you and bombard your mind with its ever accusing thoughts.

I found that many Christians today do not know what Bible forgiveness is and therefore are not successful at practicing it. If you leave unforgiveness in your heart for any length of time, it will cause a root of bitterness. These roots of bitterness are extremely life-crushing and destroy many people from the inside out. All of us must deal with unforgiveness and the things that cause it in us before it gets a death grip on our very lives.

"Looking diligently lest any man fail of the grace of

31

> *God; lest any root of **bitterness** springing up trouble*
> *you, and thereby many be defiled . . ."*
>
> Hebrews 12:15

Jesus Himself dealt with this and taught His disciples very clearly what they must do. He instructed Peter, who must have had plenty of reasons to be in unforgiveness, to forgive his offending brother seventy times seven all in the same day. One must have a lot of rascals for friends if he is being sinned against this many times in the same day. However, you must forgive even the same person for their repeated offenses against you. This alone could keep you very busy throughout your life's course here on the earth. But believe me, friend, it is worth it.

> *"Then came Peter to him, and said, Lord, how oft*
> *shall my brother sin against me, and I forgive him?*
> *till seven times?*
>
> *Jesus saith unto him, I say not unto thee, Until seven*
> *times: but, Until **seventy** times seven."*
>
> Matthew 18:21-22

The very best and swiftest way to get over the hurt or ill feeling toward others is to forgive them. Until you forgive them, they will live with you in your mind and rob you of strength and inner joy. Until you forgive them, they will be part of your meditation times and will be in your prayers. You cannot get rid of someone until you can get them out of your head and heart.

Unforgiveness, hurt, resentment, anger, bitterness, and prejudice will only feed your mental anguish and affect your motivation and zeal. They will distort your ability to reason and decay your self-esteem. You must do something immediately to forgive those who offend you, especially if they are brothers or sisters in the Lord.

Until you truly forgive someone, you will not get free from them. Every time you see them at the restaurant or shopping mall, you will be reminded of all they have said or did against you. Who wants to live this way?

Forgiving someone doesn't mean you are totally free from the effect of the offense or healed from its pain. This mistake is common among men. Just because I forgive you doesn't mean I want to be your best friend. In fact, what you did to me may separate us from intimate fellowship for now or forever (but not in strife or ill feelings).

Just because I have forgiven you doesn't mean all is forgotten (that's another mistake made often). You see, to forgive simply means to drop the charges. It doesn't mean I have healed to the degree that I want to be with you. You offended me or sinned against me and I forgive you. Now don't rub it under my nose. Give me time away from you to finish the healing process and reestablish that part of my life.

If I forgive you, that means I drop all charges against you. I will never bring it up again. I will tell no other person about it. I will not be prejudiced against you. I will not turn others against you. I will not persecute you or prosecute you in any way whatsoever because I have chosen to forgive you.

Time in itself is not a healer, but it does take time to heal. Every so often you get an instant healing, inside or out, but normally it is a recovery system. I don't believe that if you just give something enough time it will be cured or just go away. That's not always true. In fact, seldom is this true. Many things must be confronted and dealt with before they go away.

In many people's lives, time only makes it worse. The longer they take to drop the charges, the more they talk against their offender and the deeper the hurt goes.

The moment you give up your pursuit to pay back and get even and seek restitution, the sooner your own healing begins. I've known people who even got an outstanding bodily healing attached to their forgiving someone. Forgiveness is a choice and one you and I must exercise, as painful and taxing as it may be.

Let me help you here. Don't dig up any old graves you don't have to. Let that which is dead be dead and that which is buried be buried. The Word of God will help you bring up offenses and violations of old and lead you to releasing those who maimed your life. Let Him do it with you.

Many times it isn't even necessary to go to the person who hurt you years ago. Sometimes for their own sake you must go to them so they can be free from the criminal act they waged against you. Just like unforgiveness is a wicked thing and everyone loses when we hold onto it, so forgiveness is a powerful thing and everyone wins when we do it.

I must say here that there is a time when you must go to the authorities of your life and report criminal acts against you or tell your story. There is a time when this will literally stop the continual offender and protect others from their aggression, but be reminded that this is very rare and should only be practiced by the Christian as a last resort.

A whole book could be written on this subject alone. Please meditate on the following scriptures until you have peace about living in instant forgiveness every day of your life.

*"Take heed to yourselves: If thy brother trespass against thee, **rebuke** him; and if he repent, forgive him.*

And if he trespass against thee seven times in a day, and seven times in a day turn again to thee, saying, I repent; thou shalt forgive him."

Luke 17:3-4

"Therefore is the kingdom of heaven likened unto a certain king, which would take account of his servants.

And when he had begun to reckon, one was brought unto him, which owed him ten thousand talents.

But forasmuch as he had not to pay, his lord commanded him to be sold, and his wife, and children, and all that he had, and payment to be made.

The servant therefore fell down, and worshipped him, saying, Lord, have patience with me, and I will pay thee all.

Then the lord of that servant was moved with compassion, and loosed him, and forgave him the debt.

But the same servant went out, and found one of his fellow servants, which owed him an hundred pence: and he laid hands on him, and took him by the throat, saying, Pay me that thou owest.

And his fellowservant fell down at his feet, and besought him, saying, Have patience with me, and I will pay thee all.

And he would not: but went and cast him into prison,

till he should pay the debt.

So when his fellowservants saw what was done, they were very sorry, and came and told unto their lord all that was done.

Then his lord, after that he had called him, said unto him, O thou wicked servant, I forgave thee all that debt, because thou desiredst me:

Shouldest not thou also have had compassion on thy fellowservant, even as I had pity on thee?

And his lord was wroth, and delivered him to the tormentors, till he should pay all that was due unto him.

So likewise shall my heavenly Father do also unto you, if ye from your hearts forgive not every one his brother their trespasses."

Matthew 18:23-35

*"Blessed are ye, when men shall **revile** you, and persecute you, and shall say all manner of evil against you falsely, for my sake.*

Rejoice, and be exceeding glad: for great is your reward in heaven: for so persecuted they the prophets which were before you."

Matthew 5:11-12

"And when they were come to the place, which is called Calvary, there they crucified him, and the malefactors, one on the right hand, and the other on the left.

*Then said Jesus, Father, **forgive** them; for they know not what they do. And they parted his raiment, and cast lots."*

Luke 23:33-34

"For out of much affliction and anguish of heart I wrote unto you with many tears; not that ye should be grieved, but that ye might know the love which I have more abundantly unto you.

But if any have caused grief, he hath not grieved me, but in part: that I may not overcharge you all.

Sufficient to such a man is this punishment, which was inflicted of many.

*So that contrariwise ye ought rather to **forgive** him, and comfort him, lest perhaps such a one should be swallowed up with overmuch sorrow.*

Wherefore I beseech you that ye would confirm your love toward him.

For to this end also did I write, that I might know the proof of you, whether ye be obedient in all things.

To whom ye forgive any thing, I forgive also: for if I forgave any thing, to whom I forgave it, for your sakes forgave I it in the person of Christ;

Lest Satan should get an advantage of us: for we are not ignorant of his devices."

2 Corinthians 2:4-11

CHAPTER 7
DON'T PERMIT IT—
DON'T ALLOW IT

Dr. Lester Sumrall (one of the Kingdom's greatest statesmen) once told me, "Don't be afraid to make them mad when you preach!" "Be bold," he added. "Why?" I asked. "Because," he said, "God's people (especially Americans) don't seem to do hardly anything until they get mad. When they get mad, they will put their foot down and yell 'that's enough!'"

There comes a time in even passive people's lives when they have had enough. When enough is enough, then it's time to fight. This is good, but it's not good enough. We must put our foot down against our enemies way before they get a foothold in our life. I refuse to fellowship with any of my enemies. I am not even going to have conversations with them. I command them, in Jesus' name, to shut up, and I forcefully drive them from my life. No way am I going to let depression, discouragement, fear, or any other enemy hang around me.

Don't flirt with your enemies, and don't let them flirt with you. Deal with them right now. As the old saying goes, "nip it in the bud." The minute you start feeling or sensing the presence of that thing that harms you, begin then to resist it. Use your five senses to recognize these things coming upon you as well as your inner feelings and thoughts. Examining your thoughts will tell you a lot about a battle that is about to come upon you. Ask God to give you keen discernment to spot these perpetrators of your soul before they can set in.

It's like a headache coming on. If you do something about it when you first feel it or even suspect it, then normally it never sets in as a crippling enemy to ruin your day or slow your functioning ability. This is not at all difficult for a person to do, but it does take some training effort so you will be quick to respond next time and eventually without even thinking about it. Man, the devil hates this kind of person.

> *"But we are not of them who draw back unto perdition; but of them that believe to the saving of the soul."*
>
> Hebrews 10:39

Too many people draw back and slow down, especially when they are going through pressure and stressful things. I've learned over the years that it is actually easier to press in to the things of God than it is to pull away. I know for some that is a strange statement to make. It is hard to believe if you are one who normally pulls back and slacks off. I'm telling you that this very practice of pulling back and slacking off is part of your problem.

Right when they need the strength of Christian fellowship and the encouragement of our God, many people pull away. Many go home and stay. What a shame. What a crippling effect this will have on them the rest of their life.

> *"Let not your heart be troubled: ye believe in God, believe also in me."*
>
> John 14:1

This small statement spoken by Jesus was certainly not small talk. He meant every word of it. It puts the responsibility of our heart condition on you and me. We always want to blame the devil for things or point to and blame others. I know there is a time when your enemy is guilty of causing you pain and damage, but he is not the steward of your heart.

It is your inner man, and they are your feelings, and God is telling *you* to do something about protecting them.

Do not let your heart be troubled! "Do not let" (or allow) means that I have a choice whether or not it is going to happen. The Bible says not to allow it. I always say: don't permit it and don't allow it.

> *"Do not allow what you consider good to be spoken of as evil."*
>
> Romans 14:16 (NIV)

There it is again. The Holy Scriptures are instructing us to give no permission or allowance for things to be evil spoken of. Never let the devil, or for that matter any person, to put down what you believe or any part of your Christianity. If you meditate on the things that are good, you can't help but feel better. If you think about the things that bother you, then even the Word of God seems to be too small to help you.

Don't allow people to speak bad things over your life. Don't allow your mind to do it either.

> *"For if our heart **condemn** us, God is greater than our heart, and knoweth all things.*
>
> *Beloved, if our heart condemn us not, then have we confidence toward God."*
>
> 1 John 3:20-21

41

*"Hast thou faith? have it to thyself before God. Happy is he that **condemneth** not himself in that thing which he alloweth."*

Romans 14:22

Stop condemning yourself. Stop being so hard on yourself. Stop putting yourself down. Stop thinking all the time about what others say about you. Stop thinking all the time about what others think about you. Don't permit it! Don't allow it!

Learn that what people think and say is really none of your concern. There is little if anything you can do about it. But you can guard your heart and your head from it.

What if you blow it? So, you've blown it before. Who hasn't? Get back up again, in fact, again and again and again.

The scriptures that follow teach us to encourage ourselves in the Lord. I refer to this truth so often in my life and ministry because it is the very survival of my soul, my peace of mind. There are just those times when no one is around to encourage you or maybe wouldn't even know how if they were.

*"And the people, the men of Israel, **encouraged** themselves, and set their battle again in array in the place where they put themselves in array the first day."*

Judges 20:22

"And David was greatly distressed; for the people spake of stoning him, because the soul of all the people was grieved, every man for his sons and for his daughters: but David encouraged himself in the LORD his God."

1 Samuel 30:6

CHAPTER 8
STRONGHOLDS, IMAGINATIONS, AND THOUGHTS

"(For the weapons of our warfare are not carnal, but mighty through God to the pulling down of strong holds;)

Casting down imaginations, and every high thing that exalteth itself against the knowledge of God, and bringing into captivity every thought to the obedience of Christ . . ."

2 Corinthians 10:4-5

You must realize that you have enemies but also that you have weapons that are more than human. In fact, they are powerful through God. They are not powerful in themselves, but through God they are.

We are not weak, but we are strong if we battle through God. You must include God in all that you do and even what you think.

These verses in Corinthians remind us that it's more than possible to put our enemies down and overpower them.

I believe that these verses relate to our minds. I see the

strongholds as habits in our lives. For example, if you smoke cigarettes, you are really doing two things. You are actually giving way to your mind which tells you that you must have a smoke. Then you follow that strong thought and actually light up and allow the drug of nicotine to enter your system.

When you quit smoking, you are doing two things. You never allow nicotine to enter your body, and you constantly pull down the stronghold that speaks to you so loudly to have a cigarette. As a matter of fact, your mind will tell you that you will die of a nicotine fit if you don't get a cigarette soon. This is a lie. Actually you are probably aiding in your death whenever you light up.

> *"Because the carnal mind is **enmity** against God: for it is not subject to the law of God, neither indeed can be."*
>
> Romans 8:7

You must understand that your mind is actually enmity against God until it is renewed by the Word of God. To me, a renewed mind is one that has had all strongholds pulled down and thinks the thoughts of God now. It agrees with the Word of God and doesn't even entertain imaginations.

Do not put up with these strongholds (convincing habits) in your mind. Use the Word of God and your prayer life to pull them down. I have personally and permanently pulled down the strongholds of smoking, drinking, anger, temper tantrums, cussing, and fighting. What have you beaten?

If you beat the enemy in your mind, you have beaten the enemy. No, I'm not making light of demon activity or the influence of evil forces in people's lives. Sure there is a devil and demons, but they can't even clearly talk to you once you've turned your mind off from them.

I know that I am making myself vulnerable by saying these things, but it is worth it. It is worth it to be criticized by my critics in order to help you finally be free and victorious.

It is not just mind over matter. It is the Word of God renewing your mind that helps you overcome. When I quit smoking, I tried in my own might several times, all to little avail. But when I used the Word of God to meditate in, I forcefully pulled down that habit in my mind. When my mind was convinced that I was done smoking, the battle became very easy. Getting nicotine out of my blood was very easy after I beat the strongholds in my mind.

This is why so many people cast out demons and bind the devil and still don't get free. Some actually go for deliverance, but after a short time they return to their habit or stronghold. If you have a demon, go for deliverance, but if you have a stronghold, then learn how to cast it down.

Many people try to cast down satan or demons. Sure, there is a time for spiritual warfare. I'm not refuting that. I am saying, though, that most likely the battle is in your mind. You *cast out* demons, but you *cast down* imaginations and *pull down* strongholds.

Sure, there are fiery darts or wicked thoughts shot into us by the evil one and also by the words of evil people. Even good people who love you could at times say something that would not be good for you to hear. However, realize that these fiery darts always come in seed form; they in themselves are not yet strongholds.

45

Let God anoint His Word in your life. Find scriptures that address what you are dealing with and meditate in them constantly until you are free. Then go on and cast down another stronghold. One after the other you will see God help you by renewing your mind and giving you power over these controlling thoughts.

> ". . . and bringing into captivity every thought to the obedience of Christ . . ."
>
> 2 Corinthians 10:5

Notice here that every thought that exalts itself against the Word of God must be dealt with. You can't do this by casting out demons or even binding them. You must deal with every thought and the thinking process that convinces you that the Word is not working for you or that it is not strong enough to free you.

Many people say they cannot quit smoking. They have *convinced themselves*. But when you turn the Word of God loose in your mind, you will overpower the thoughts and pin them down. You will pull down strongholds and cast down imaginations and begin to see your freedom.

You must use the Word of God and involve the Spirit of God because meditation and mind control are just not enough. Your thoughts, or trying to control them through mere determination or resistance, will not be powerful enough to win.

Are you not convinced yet? Is your stronghold stopping you from receiving this simple truth? Read these other scriptures about your thoughts and let them enter in.

> "But when Jesus perceived their **thoughts**, he answering said unto them, What reason ye in your hearts?"
>
> Luke 5:22

*"And he said unto them, Why are ye troubled? and why do **thoughts** arise in your hearts?"*

Luke 24:38

*"Which shew the work of the law written in their hearts, their conscience also bearing witness, and their **thoughts** the mean while accusing or else excusing one another . . ."*

Romans 2:15

*"For the word of God is quick, and powerful, and sharper than any twoedged sword, piercing even to the dividing asunder of soul and spirit, and of the joints and marrow, and is a discerner of the **thoughts** and intents of the heart."*

Hebrews 4:12

CHAPTER 9
BIBLE ANTIDOTES

BIBLE WAYS TO GET HEALED INSIDE AND WAR MENTAL WARFARE

1. Learn to live a fasted life.

"Is not this the fast that I have chosen? to loose the bands of wickedness, to undo the heavy burdens, and to let the oppressed go free, and that ye break every yoke?

Is it not to deal thy bread to the hungry, and that thou bring the poor that are cast out to thy house? when thou seest the naked, that thou cover him; and that thou hide not thyself from thine own flesh?

Then shall thy light break forth as the morning, and thine health shall spring forth speedily: and thy righteousness shall go before thee; the glory of the LORD shall be thy rereward."

Isaiah 58:6-8

Fasting is one way to free yourself as well as get God on the scene. Study these scriptures and learn the kind of fast that God honors.

2. Get your soul anchored as quickly as possible and

keep it that way for the rest of your life.

> *"Wherein God, willing more abundantly to shew unto the heirs of promise the immutability of his counsel, confirmed it by an oath:*
>
> *That by two immutable things, in which it was impossible for God to lie, we might have a strong consolation, who have fled for refuge to lay hold upon the hope set before us:*
>
> *Which hope we have as an anchor of the soul, both sure and stedfast, and which entereth into that within the veil . . ."*

Hebrews 6:17-19

It is the personal responsibility of every Christian to anchor his own soul. Your soul, remember, is your feelings, your intellect, your emotions, and your will. These all must be anchored in the Kingdom of God through the systems of God, or sooner or later something or someone will lead you astray. Tithing, attending church, Bible study, and prayer will all cause your soul to be anchored.

3. Abstain from fleshly lusts and things that make you feel guilty.

> *"Dearly beloved, I beseech you as strangers and pilgrims, abstain from fleshly lusts, which war against the soul . . ."*

1 Peter 2:11

Abstaining from fleshly lusts can free your soul. Actually, by abstaining from these things you don't cripple your soul in the first place. The less your soul is hurt and burdened, the less you need healing. Protect yourself.

4. You should start now to renew your mind.

> *"I beseech you therefore, brethren, by the mercies of God, that ye present your bodies a living sacrifice, holy, acceptable unto God, which is your reasonable service.*
>
> *And be not conformed to this world: but be ye transformed by the renewing of your mind, that ye may prove what is that good, and acceptable, and perfect, will of God."*
>
> Romans 12:1-2

Every single day you and I must work at renewing our mind. This special washing effect is what cleanses away the pollutants of the world from our thinking processes. They also wash away the contaminants that are on us that cause us to worry, fear, doubt, and quit.

Refuse to allow anything or anybody to conform you to the spirit or the ways of the world. Do not conform but be transformed.

5. Take a good inventory of your relationships.

> *"Do not be deceived: 'Evil **company** corrupts good habits.'"*
>
> 1 Corinthians 15:33 (NKJ)

Over and over the Bible teaches us to watch carefully our company and choose our friends with discretion. Whom you are around a lot is whom you begin to act like. Whom you listen to is whom you eventually sound like. Don't ever hurt anybody or hate anybody. You can clean up your relationships without aggressively going after any people. But I cannot express enough the value of guarding who your friends are.

6. Practice thinking right and on the right things.

*"Finally, brethren, whatsoever things are true, what-soever things are honest, whatsoever things are just, whatsoever things are pure, whatsoever things are lovely, whatsoever things are of good report; if there be any virtue, and if there be any praise, **think on these things.**"*

Philippians 4:8

If you are going to live daily in peace, you must learn what to think upon and force yourself to do it. The Bible lists for us here in these verses the things we should concentrate on. Do it. Tell yourself to do it. It doesn't just happen.

7. Do something with your affections and your emotions.

*"Set your affection on **things above**, not on things on the earth."*

Colossians 3:2

*"Thou wilt keep him in **perfect peace**, whose mind is stayed on thee: because he trusteth in thee.*

Trust ye in the LORD for ever: for in the LORD JEHO-VAH is everlasting strength . . ."

Isaiah 26:3-4

You have to practice setting your affections on things above. Slowly, though, as you put these principles into practice, you will crave to look up and look on Jesus, the Author and Finisher of our faith. Living in a peaceful environment is wonderful, but living in inner peace is even more grand. There really is a way to live without hurt and darkness.

8. Develop a system of purposed meditation.

"But his delight is in the law of the LORD; and in his law doth he meditate day and night.

And he shall be like a tree planted by the rivers of water, that bringeth forth his fruit in his season; his leaf also shall not wither; and whatsoever he doeth shall prosper."

Psalm 1:2-3

*"**Meditate** upon these things; give thyself wholly to them; that thy profiting may appear to all."*

1 Timothy 4:15

Meditation is a real key to having a strong soul. A good mental attitude comes from meditating on good things. If you constantly rehearse things that hurt and disappoint you, you will be in gloominess and even despair. But if you learn to rehearse the things that have blessed you, you will feel blessed. If you take time to slowly meditate on the Scriptures and the promises of God, then you will feel strength come.

9. Pay attention to yourself and refuse to drift through life.

"Take heed unto thyself, and unto the doctrine; continue in them: for in doing this thou shalt both save thyself, and them that hear thee."

1 Timothy 4:16

Taking heed to your lifestyle, your friends, and how you spend your time and money, all have to do with a profitable or not so profitable life. Also your doctrines (what you believe) and whether or not you are living according to them affect the outcome of your situations. "Take heed" simply means to pay attention to. Pay attention and assure that you are living out your life according to these things.

Then you will not only be profitable, but others will see it.

10. Get control of your money.

"My son, if thou be surety for thy friend, if thou hast stricken thy hand with a stranger,

*Thou art **snared** with the words of thy mouth, thou art taken with the words of thy mouth."*

Proverbs 6:1-2

*"For the love of money is the root of all evil: which while some coveted after, they have erred from the faith, and pierced themselves through with many **sorrows**."*

1 Timothy 6:10

Many people live a self-afflicted life. They constantly shoot themselves in the foot. Your finances are a key part of your living in good mental health. Budget and discipline your spending so whether you've got a lot or a little you feel in charge of your situation instead of a victim of it.

11. Get control of your mouth.

*"The wicked is **snared** by the transgression of his lips: but the just shall come out of trouble.*

A man shall be satisfied with good by the fruit of his mouth: and the recompence of a man's hands shall be rendered unto him."

Proverbs 12:13-14

Nobody listens more to what you say than you yourself. Your ears pick up what you say, even when you are by yourself. Start right now to change your mouth. You will fail at first, but when you do, bounce right back. Soon you will be saying good, positive, and wholesome things that encourage you and others.

12. Encourage yourself in the Lord.

*"And the people, the men of Israel, **encouraged** themselves, and set their battle again in array in the place where they put themselves in array the first day."*

Judges 20:22

*"And David was greatly distressed; for the people spake of stoning him, because the soul of all the people was grieved, every man for his sons and for his daughters: but David **encouraged** himself in the LORD his God."*

1 Samuel 30:6

Everybody alive has bad days, from bad hair days to real crises. Each of us must build within us a means by which we deal with these daily disappointments. Find encouraging and empowering scriptures in your Bible, and underline them and mark them somehow so you can find them again in a hurry, perhaps in the night season or during a crisis. Once you establish a system in your life to encourage yourself in the Lord, you will almost always refer to it automatically. You will also be one of those who encourages others without even trying.

13. Pray in the Spirit.

"But ye, beloved, building up yourselves on your most holy faith, praying in the Holy Ghost,

Keep yourselves in the love of God, looking for the mercy of our Lord Jesus Christ unto eternal life."

Jude 20-21

One of the greatest gifts given to man by the Lord Jesus is the gift of our personal prayer language. Praying in the Spirit is powerful, and it builds you up. Don't settle for depression and discouragement when you can have joy and self-esteem. God gave you the gift to do it. Do it. You will feel your strength rising almost immediately.

14. *Spend* time with God.

*"Repent ye therefore, and be converted, that your sins may be blotted out, when the times of refreshing shall come from the **presence of the Lord** . . ."*

Acts 3:19

*"Thou wilt shew me the path of life: in thy presence is **fulness of joy**; at thy right hand there are pleasures for evermore."*

Psalm 16:11

The more time you spend in prayer talking and listening to God, the more joy you will have. Joy is an automatic by-product of being in His presence. You can't pray too much. Even if all your petitions do not come to pass when you think they should, you will still feel good about His presence. There is nothing like it.

15. Forgive everybody as quickly as you can.

For your own sake be sure that you forgive everyone as quickly as you can. The quicker you forgive your offender, the faster you get healed. You can't feel good about yourself when you are harboring unforgiveness, hurt, and bitterness. Don't permit yourself the carnal treat of holding grudges.

CHAPTER 10
JESUS IS ANOINTED TO HEAL YOUR HEART

You must come to grips with the fact that only the anointing of God can totally and absolutely set you free from the burdens and yokes that strap your life. Professionals, medicines, stimulants, and the such may aid you for a season but won't heal you permanently. These things are there to help you cope, to comfort you while you go through the storms of life. But the anointing that is on Jesus is there to totally set you free, not cope with but conquer your enemies, even the enemies of your soul.

> *"It shall come to pass in that day that his burden will be taken away from your shoulder, and his yoke from your neck, and the yoke will be destroyed because of the **anointing** oil."*

> Isaiah 10:27 (NKJ)

Jesus is the One who is anointed by God to free you. He is the One and the Way whom God Himself chose to heal you, save you, and deliver you. Only Jesus has such an assignment and power to touch your life in such a way. There is no other anointing but this anointing that can help you this way.

> *"Surely He has borne our griefs and carried our sorrows; yet we esteemed Him stricken, smitten by God, and afflicted.*
>
> *But He was wounded for our transgressions, He was bruised for our iniquities; the chastisement for our peace was upon Him, and by His **stripes** we are healed."*
>
> Isaiah 53:4-5 (NKJ)

Notice that these scriptures tell us that Jesus not only bought healing for our bodies but also for our souls. That's right, even Calvary provides for the healing of the inner man.

Surely He has borne our griefs and carried our sorrows. He took upon Himself our soul battles and the things that hurt us inside. The whole price was paid, not part of it. The work was finished at Calvary, not partially finished. The sacrifice was for the whole man, not just the house (body) that he lives in. Jesus literally laid down His life that you and I might be saved from everything, all of our enemies—*all* of them.

Jesus was and is the Christ, the Anointed One. The name Christ literally means "the Anointed One and His anointing." Christ is not Jesus' last name as some suppose. It is His title. You could literally say "Jesus, the Anointed One and His anointing."

It's the presence and the anointing of this Christ that sets us free. It is now our responsibility to set others free. It is the key to the Kingdom that will let you live with joy and great peace.

> *"The Spirit of the Lord God is upon Me, because the Lord has **anointed** Me to preach good tidings to the*

poor; He has sent Me to heal the brokenhearted, to proclaim liberty to the captives, and the opening of the prison to those who are bound;

To proclaim the acceptable year of the LORD, and the day of vengeance of our God; to comfort all who mourn,

To console those who mourn in Zion, to give them beauty for ashes, the oil of joy for mourning, the garment of praise for the spirit of heaviness; that they may be called trees of righteousness, the planting of the LORD, that He may be glorified."

Isaiah 61:1-3 (NKJ)

*" 'The Spirit of the LORD is upon Me, because He has **anointed** Me to preach the gospel to the poor; He has sent Me to heal the brokenhearted, to proclaim liberty to the captives and recovery of sight to the blind, to set at liberty those who are oppressed . . .' "*

Luke 4:18 (NKJ)

*"But He was wounded for our transgressions, He was bruised for our iniquities; the chastisement for our peace was upon Him, and by His **stripes** we are healed."*

Isaiah 53:5 (NKJ)

". . . To preach the acceptable year of the Lord."

Luke 4:19

*". . . how God **anointed** Jesus of Nazareth with the Holy Spirit and with power, who went about doing good and healing all who were oppressed by the devil, for God was with Him."*

Acts 10:38 (NKJ)

"Now He who establishes us with you in Christ and has anointed us is God . . ."

2 Corinthians 1:21 (NKJ)

". . . who Himself bore our sins in His own body on the tree, that we, having died to sins, might live for righteousness—by whose stripes you were healed."

1 Peter 2:24 (NKJ)

*"But you have an **anointing** from the Holy One, and you know all things.*

*But the **anointing** which you have received from Him abides in you, and you do not need that anyone teach you; but as the same anointing teaches you concerning all things, and is true, and is not a lie, and just as it has taught you, you will abide in Him."*

1 John 2:20, 27 (NKJ)

CHAPTER 11
THE HELMET OF SALVATION

"Finally, my brethren, be strong in the Lord, and in the power of his might.

Put on the whole armour of God, that ye may be able to stand against the wiles of the devil.

For we wrestle not against flesh and blood, but against principalities, against powers, against the rulers of the darkness of this world, against spiritual wickedness in high places.

Wherefore take unto you the whole armour of God, that ye may be able to withstand in the evil day, and having done all, to stand.

Stand therefore, having your loins girt about with truth, and having on the breastplate of righteousness;

And your feet shod with the preparation of the gospel of peace;

Above all, taking the shield of faith, wherewith ye shall be able to quench all the fiery darts of the wicked.

And take the helmet of salvation, and the sword of the Spirit, which is the word of God:

Praying always with all prayer and supplication in the Spirit, and watching thereunto with all perseverance and supplication for all saints . . ."

Ephesians 6:10-18

It is of utmost importance that you do something to protect your mind, your thinking faculties, and your ability to reason. Even though you are a Christian, it doesn't mean that you can live loosely and unprotected. It is meant that even we Christians protect ourselves from the affairs of this life.

The best way to protect yourself is to put on the helmet of salvation. This is the purposed attention and realization that one is saved and is expected by the Savior to live by His Christian principles, convictions, and Scriptures.

Each time you go to the Word of God you put on the helmet. Each time you take worry and fear to the Bible to compare it, you put on the helmet. Each time you meditate in the Word of God, especially on specific scriptures, you put on the helmet of your salvation. Each time you say to your circumstances, "What would Jesus do?" or "What should I do now that I am a Christian?" you are putting on the helmet.

The helmet of your salvation is not a piece of pretend armor that you read about and take for granted that it automatically works for you. No, you must do something every day and sometimes every hour to put it on. Praise God though that we can do it. The moment that helmet is in place you begin to think the thoughts of God. You begin to think like a Word man or Word woman. You begin to judge every thought and deal with every worry, fear, and emotion according to what the Word of God says. Amen!

Without the helmet of salvation you will think like a mere man. You could compare your thoughts with any sinner's thoughts, and they will be very close to the same. It's that helmet of salvation, that Christlike reasoning, that begins to change your mind.

I've said for years that most people are notorious for consistently making the wrong decisions and dealing with things the wrong way. You cannot go by human wisdom or some little thing you learned by listening to others. You cannot go by the stars or superstition. You have to go by the Word of God.

Do not permit yourself to be led by yourself or any other human reasoning. We are of Christ and His divine nature, not of the world or its ways.

> *"But let us, who are of the day, be sober, putting on the breastplate of faith and love; and for an **helmet**, the hope of salvation."*

> 1 Thessalonians 5:8

This verse reminds us of the element of the helmet that we are supposed to put on. Almost everywhere the helmet is mentioned it is accompanied with the action needed by the Christian to put it on.

The helmet is our Christian hope. When you deal with things that seem hopeless or you feel hopeless while you are dealing with them, you will most likely lose. But if you deal with things according to the truth, then you will almost always win, and you will fight with hope in God and His Word until the battle is over.

There is a big difference between fighting and dealing with the issues of life with the helmet and without it.

*"For who hath known the mind of the Lord, that he may instruct him? But we have the **mind of Christ**."*

1 Corinthians 2:16

You have the mind of Christ. You have access to the mind of Christ whenever you wish. All you have to do is go to the Bible and find His Word on the matter that you are dealing with and then meditate in it until you get that revelation knowledge that you need to solve the problem. When that revelation knowledge comes, the hope to win comes with it. It really is that simple.

*"And be **renewed** in the spirit of your mind . . ."*

Ephesians 4:23

"I beseech you therefore, brethren, by the mercies of God, that ye present your bodies a living sacrifice, holy, acceptable unto God, which is your reasonable service.

*And be not conformed to this world: but be ye transformed by the **renewing** of your mind, that ye may prove what is that good, and acceptable, and perfect will of God."*

Romans 12:1-2

May I remind you that you must be always working on renewing your mind. The renewing of your mind is a continual process of washing your thoughts with the Word of God. This slowly changes your mind, and you begin to think like the Bible, like Christ.

Don't get into the habit of only running to the Word of God during times of battle or times of trouble. Go to the Word often, in fact constantly, and use it as preventive medicine. Be ready to respond with the mind of Christ, the renewed mind, the Word, before the battle comes.

Learn to fellowship with people who are of like precious faith. Sup with those whom you are trying to evangelize, but fellowship with those who are of the Word of God. That way you will always be talking about the Word and how each other fought and won the battles of life. This is so valuable. If you will just think about it for a minute, you will realize that you always come away from those conversations that were filled with doubt and worry with a troubled spirit and a feeling of being down. Not so when you walk away from a time of hearing testimonies or truths.

Renew your mind daily. Put on the Word of God daily. Wash your mind with the Word of God daily. Put on the mind of Christ daily. It will cause your path to be sure and your strength to always increase. You will think clearly, and you will be ready mentally to face anything that comes your way whether it is expected or a shock to you.

PRAYER OF SALVATION

YOU CAN BE SAVED FROM ETERNAL DAMNA-TION and get God's help now in this life. All you have to do is humble your heart, believe in Christ's work at Calvary for you, and pray the prayer below.

"Dear Heavenly Father,

I know that I have sinned and fallen short of Your expectations of me. I have come to realize that I cannot run my own life. I do not want to continue the way I've been living, neither do I want to face an eternity of torment and damnation.

I know that the wages of sin is death, but I can be spared from this through the gift of the Lord Jesus Christ. I believe that He died for me, and I receive His provision now. I will not be ashamed of Him, and I will tell all my friends and family members that I have made this wonderful decision.

Dear Lord Jesus,

Come into my heart now and live in me and be my Savior, Master, and Lord. I will do my very best to chase after You and to learn Your ways by submitting to a pastor, reading my Bible, going to a church that preaches about **You**, and keeping sin out of my life.

I also ask You to give me the power to be healed from any sickness and disease and to deliver me from those things that have me bound.

I love You and thank You for having me, and I am eagerly looking forward to a long, beautiful relationship with You."

Books by Mark T. Barclay

Beware of Seducing Spirits

This is not a book on demonology. It is a book about the misbehavior of men and women and the seducing and deceiving spirits that influence them to do what they do. Brother Barclay exposes the most prominent seducing spirits of the last days.

Beware of the Sin of Familiarity

This book is a scriptural study on the most devastating sin in the Body of Christ today. The truths in this book will make you aware of this excess familiarity and reveal to you some counterattacks.

Building a Supernatural Church

A guide to pioneering, organizing, and establishing a new local church. This is a fast-reading, simple, instructional guide to leaders and helps people who are working together to build the Church.

Charging the Year 2000

This book will remind you of the last-days' promises of God as well as alert you to the many snares and falsehoods with which satan will try to deceive and seduce last-days' believers. "A handbook for living in the '90s."

Enduring Hardness

God has called His Church an army and the believers, soldiers. It is mandatory that all Christians endure hardness as good soldiers of Jesus Christ. This book will help build more backbone in you.

How to Avoid Shipwreck

A book of preventive medicine, helping people stay strong and full of faith. You will be strengthened by this book as you learn how to anchor your soul.

How to Relate to Your Pastor

It is very important in these last days that God's people understand the office of pastor. As we put into practice these principles, the Church will grow in numbers and also increase its vision for the world.

How to Always Reap a Harvest

In this book Brother Barclay explains the principles that make believers successful and fruitful. It shows you how to live a better life and become far more productive and enjoy a full harvest.

Improving Your Performance

Every Christian everywhere needs to read this book. Even leaders will be challenged by this writing. It will help tremendously in the organization and unity of your ministry and working force.

The Making of a Man of God

In this book you'll find some of the greatest, yet simplest, insights to becoming a man or woman of God and to launching your ministry with accuracy and credibility. The longevity of your ministry will be enhanced by the truths herein. You will learn the difference between being a convert, an epistle, a disciple, and a minister.

Preachers of Righteousness

This is not a book for pulpiteers or reverends only but for all of us. It reveals the real ministry style of Jesus Christ and the sold-out commitment of His followers—the most powerful, awesome force on the face of the earth.

The Real Truth About Tithing

This book is a thorough study of God's Word on tithing, which will fully inform believers how to tithe biblically and accurately. You will be armed with the truth, and your life will never be the same!

The Remnant Church

God has always had a people and will always have a people. Brother Barclay speaks of the upcoming revival and how we can be those who are alive and remain when our Master returns.

Sheep, Goats, Wolves

A scriptural yet practical explanation of human behavior in our local churches and how church leaders and members can deal with each other. You will especially enjoy the tests that are in the back of this book.

The Sin of Lawlessness

Lawlessness always challenges authority and ultimately is designed to hurt people. This book will convict those who are in lawlessness and warn those who could be future victims. It will help your life and straighten your walk with Him.

Basic Christian Handbook (minibook)

This mini book is packed full of scriptures and basic information needed for a solid Christian foundation. It would make an inexpensive and effective tract and is a must for new converts. Many church workers are using it for altar counseling.

The Captain's Mantle (minibook)

Something happened in the cave Adullum. Find out how 400 distressed, indebted, and discontented men came out of that cave as one of the most awesome armies in history.